Whiskers' Halloween

BY SHANA GORIAN

Whiskers' Halloween
A Cat Named Whiskers
Copyright©2024 Shana Gorian. All rights reserved.

All rights reserved under International and Pan American Copyright conventions. No part of this book may be reproduced, transmitted, downloaded, recorded, or stored in any information storage and retrieval system, in any form or by any means, whether electronic or mechanical, now known or hereinafter invented, without the express written permission of the publisher, except for brief quotations for review purposes.

Written by Shana Gorian
Art by Four Fifty Six Design

First Edition, 2024

This book belongs to

In a quiet little house on a moonlit street
lived a cat named Whiskers, gentle and sweet.

One night so dark, Whiskers heard a strange noise,
one that didn't come from his house or his toys.

But he found nothing there, so what could it be?
He heard it again! It was time to go see.

Under moonlight so eerie,
he crept down the block,
pouncing from fence to tree to rock.

But he couldn't quite place the unusual sound,
so he continued to search, quietly, around.

When suddenly,
a ghost in a white sheet
screamed, "Boo!"

Whiskers dashed off to safety,
and away the ghost flew.

Next, came a witch in a pointy black hat, with a bubbling potion in a cauldron so fat.

Whiskers shivered and hid,
admitting defeat,
then scampered away
on his soft, little feet.